THE RIGHT
INTERVIEW

Series Titles by Saad E. Abbas

✓ The Right Resume and Curriculum Vitae

✓ The Right Interview

✓ The Right Virtual Meeting Etiquette

✓ The Right Risk and Crisis Management

✓ The Right Customer Service

✓ The Right Innovation and Change Management

✓ The Right Conflict Management

✓ The Right Feasibility Study

✓ The Right Business Plan Writing

✓ The Right Leadership

THE RIGHT INTERVIEW

By

Saad E. Abbas

P ISBN: 978-1-7392159-2-7
E ISBN: 978-1-7392159-3-4
Year: 2022

GULF BOOK SERVICES
Published by
Gulf Book Service Ltd
20-22 Wenlock Road, London
NI 7GU
UK
Email: info@gulfbooks.co.uk

Designed by: New Tech FZE

Consultant, Trainer, Mentor and Author

Saad E. Abbas

MBA, RACMC, CLC, CCMC, CIC, FGLC, SGC, ECMC, CCEPRM, AFIIBI, RMIFIC, DEIB (Finance), ICDL, MAD, QMS-LA, MBAD, DQA-TL, SKEA-TL, ADAGEP-TL, IAA-A, DHDA (Assessor Trainer), BIT & BLSI (ASHI), BLST & ALST (AHA), NAEMSE, MFAI & Ml (PADI), IT (ISEA), HSAI (HSA)

Degrees and Certifications:

- MBA (Financial Wealth Management) University of Hull UK.
- Risk and Crisis Management Consultant (RACMC)
- Certified Life Coach (CLC)
- Certified Career Management Coach (CCMC)
- Certified Innovation Consultant (CIC)
- Future Government Leader Consultant (FGLC)
- Smart Government Consultant (SGC)
- Event and Conference Management Consultant (ECMC)
- Certified Consultant in Electronic PR & Media (CCEPRM)
- Associate Fellow Institute of Islamic Banking & Insurance (AFIIBI)
- Risk Management Islamic Financial Institutions Consultant (RMIFC)
- Dubai Quality Award (DQA), Sheikh Khalifa Excellence Award (SKEA), Abu Dhabi Award for Excellence in Government Performance (ADAEGPTL) Team leader.

Work Experience:

- 20 Years Experience in Banks (National Bank of Dubai – ABN AMRO Bank – Barclays Bank – Emirates Bank International)
- 20 Years Experience as a Government Consultant, Trainer, Coach and Mentor

Training Programs Conducted:

1. Mastering Risk and Crisis Management
2. Mastering The Perfect Interview
3. Mastering Customer Service
4. Mastering Virtual Meeting Etiquette
5. Mastering Change Management
6. Mastering Feasibility Study
7. Mastering Conflict Management
8. Mastering Innovation Management
9. Mastering Business Plan Writing
10. Mastering Leadership

Author:

1. How to Get the Right Job in 2007
2. The Right Resume and Curriculum Vitae
3. The Right Interview
4. The Right Virtual Meeting Etiquette
5. The Right Risk and Crisis Management Plan

Chapter 1: Interview Preparation and Etiquette 1

The Interview Lists 1

1. Company Research 1

2. Advance Preparation of The Interview Questions 6

3. How To Dress For The Interview 8

4. Arriving On Time For The Interview 11

5. Waiting Room Strategies 11

6. What Not To Do During An Interview 11

7. What Should You Do During An Interview 13

Chapter 2: How to Respond to Interview Questions 17

The Two Basic Types of Tough Questions 17

Twelve of the Toughest Questions 17

1. Tell Me About Yourself? 18

2. What Are Your Strengths? 19

3. What Are Your Major Weaknesses or Limitations? 21

4. What Are Your Financial Requirements? 23

5. Why [Are You Leaving/Did You Leave] Your Present Job? 24

6. What Are Your Career Goals for the Next Five Years? 26

7. What Kind of a Position Are You Looking For? 27

8. What Accomplishment Was the Most Significant
   in Your Last Position? 28

9. Doesn't This Job Represent a Step Down from Your Last Job? 29

10. How Would You Describe Your Management Style? 29

11. How Would You Approach This Job? 30

12. Please Give Me a 360-degree Feedback from (Supervisors,
    Colleagues and Subordinates)? 31

Chapter 3: What are the Different Types of Interviews? 33

What Interviewers are Looking For? 33

Gate-Keeping Interviews: And How To Manage Them 34

The Semi-Final and Final Interviews: How to Manage Them 38

Non-Traditional Interviews: How to Manage Them 41

Chapter 4: The New Interviews Styles after COVID-19......... 47

The Changes That Have Taken Place in Interviews After COVID-19............47

A. What Virtual Meeting Platforms You Will Be Using? 48

B. Be On Time 48

C. Check Your Surroundings Before You Log In 48

D. Keep Your Eyes on The Camera 48

E. Don't be a Talking Head 49

F. Have The Right Posture 49

G. Use Headphones or Earbuds 50

1 Interview Preparation and Etiquette

Preparing for the interview is very important. I have seen many people do a great job on their Resume and "Do a Complete Blunder" on the interview. Distorting everything, they have worked hard to achieve. There are many reasons why people fail in an interview, but most of the reasons boil down to one basic reason and that is not preparing for the interview.

It does not matter how you reached the interview stage. The main thing to remember is that you have been called for the interview. What you must do next is a list of things very similar to a grocery list; you have to check each item on the list once completed.

The Interview Lists

1. Company Research

You must do a research on the company. How do you get the information? Most important what information do you need to get?

The good thing is that information is very easy to obtain currently. The invention of the Internet has forced many companies to setup web sites. This is good for you. This will enable you to go to the web page and get the information you need.

There are other ways of getting information about companies such as (company brochures—newspaper articles—economic department data—friends in the same industry—direct calling). Calling the company as a prospective client is a good idea. The sales team will give you all the information you need to know about the company.

We have talked about the how; now let us talk about the what. So, what type of information are you looking for? The information that you should focus on obtaining is the information that concerns the job you are targeting.

Example:

- Sales—look at the annual turnover of the company, sales forecasts, products, and the market conditions for the products, etc.
- Management—the departments in the company, staff motivation, expansion plans, company strategy, previous year's performance, management style, etc.
- Manufacturing—type of products, inventory management system (FIFO, LIFO, etc.), plant machinery, cost of manufacturing, product delivery channels, competition, defect percentage, etc.
- Banking—competition, services, reputation in the market, style of management, new opportunities, etc.
- Hotels—the industry, competition, location, brand name, quality of service, occupancy level, etc.
- Retail sector—product, brand name, location of retail outlets, opportunities in the market, competition, store layout, etc.

These are some of the industries that I have listed. From the above example, you can use the information on any industry and work type. You just have to dig and find the information you need. "Who said finding a job was a piece of cake?"

The following is a company fact sheet that will help you gather the information that you will need for the interview.

(Company Fact Sheet Template 1)

Skill Builder

Company Name: _____

Location: _____

Contact (People I know who work there or know the company)

Name:_____   Name: _____

Tel: _____   Tel: _____

Kind of Business: (Products and / or Services)

_____

Names of Some Typical Customers:_____

_____

_____

Significant Facts:

Annual Sales Volume: $_____

Growth Pattern (past 5 Years) _____

Number of Employees: _____   Headquarter Location: _____

Other Locations:_____

Interesting Production Statistics:_____

_____

Name of Key Manager:

Name_____   Title:_____

Name_____   Title:_____

Name_____   Title:_____

Organisation History: _____

_____

Questions to ask during the Interview:

1. _____

2. _____

3. _____

4. _____

My comments that made a positive Impact:

1. _____

2. _____

3. _____

4. _____

Comments that are not well received during the Interview:

1. _____

2. _____

3. _____

4. _____

Names of People I met:

Name_____   Title:_____

Name_____   Title:_____

Name_____   Title:_____

Items to follow through on: Date for Action

1. _____ /_____/_____

2. _____ /_____/_____

3. _____ /_____/_____

4. _____ /_____/_____

(End of Example 1:1) [1]

2. Advance preparation of the interview questions

What do you say when the interviewer asks, "Do you have any question?"

If your response is, "I cannot think of any right now" or, "I do not have any question," you are going to make a negative impression; you are likely to make the wrong impression that you are someone who is not particularly interested in the position or organisation. It could also appear that you are so desperate for a job that you will take whatever is being offered. Interviewers often use this question to gauge the depth of your motivation to get the job or your good sense in researching the organisation. It is important to plan beforehand some of the questions you will ask, if you get the opportunity to ask them.

Good questions can greatly improve the impact you make. They also help you determine whether the job is a good match for you or not.

The right frame of mind

In approaching your interviews, remember that most are a two-way street (although exceptions such as the stress interview do exist). While the interviewer needs to learn about you, to see if you are qualified, you need to determine if the job meets your needs. It is normal and expected that you will want to learn all you can about what the job opportunities are.

I recommend that you enter each interview situation with the understanding that you are there to determine whether or not the job is right for you.

The right questions to ask

The best questions to ask are those that:

- Help you determine if this is the job you want
- Make a positive impact on the interviewer
- Provide insights into what you should highlight about your background and qualifications

Questions that meet these criteria usually concern:

- What the job is like
- What the company is looking for in a candidate
- How you will fit in
- What is going on in the company

Here are some all-purpose questions as an example that you can ask:

- Whether I fill this job or not, can you tell me what your expectations are for the ins and outs of this position?
- What do you see for this company in the future – particularly as it might impact on career opportunities?
- What would I be expected to accomplish in the job we are discussing?
- What opportunities for advancement are typically available to people in this position?
- Can you tell me why this position is vacant?
- How does this position fit into the organisational structure?
- How would you describe the management philosophy of this company?
- What is this department's most important current projects?
- How much independence would I have in this job?
- How many subordinates would be under my direct supervision? Can you tell me something about these people?
- Will you please tell me about the person I would report to and other key people I would be dealing with?

Note: If you can weave these questions into an early segment of the interview, chances are you will learn what is important to the interviewer; you can then tailor your presentation accordingly.

What not to ask

What you refrain from asking an interviewer can influence the impression you make as much as what you do ask. In general, discretion in asking about compensation and fringe benefits is called for.

- It is not a good strategy to ask about benefits or retirement in an initial interview
- There are very few jobs in which salary or compensation is not of primary importance. As an applicant, you need to know what the organisation expects to pay you. This is not an item about which you need to decide whether to ask or not; it is more a matter of when to ask it.

These questions are left for the last interview with the HR Manager just before you get the offer letter.

3.   How to dress for the interview

This is one of the most important aspects of the interview that people do not seem to understand. A person's general look and the way he or she is dressed say a lot about that person. Let me explain.

If a person walks into an interview with (his or her hair not combed, or if the clothes they are wearing is wrinkled, and shabby, or if they have body odour, etc.), the interviewer will take a wrong idea about this person. It does not matter how good you are at your work, but if you cannot present yourself in a respectable manner, how will you be able to represent the company in a good way?

I have been informed that in some jobs the way you look is not important. Jobs like advertising, IT programmers and engineers are the people working in creative environments are excluded from the general rule we all must follow. **Dress in harmony with the way that those interviewing you are likely to dress.** If you are applying for a job in manufacturing where the typical dress is a sport jacket without a tie, wearing a pin-striped business suite is not appropriate. Conversely, the sport jacket is out of place when applying to a bank or financial investment firm.

Note: The thing to remember is to wear clothing just a little dressier than that required for everyday use on the job. If you would typically wear blue jeans on the job, consider interviewing in neat trousers with a shirt and jacket.

A.   How to dress

Dressing up is an art what you wear reflects your personality. Let me handle each nationality individually to make things easier.

Note: Do not wear something so striking that attention is drawn to your clothes rather than you. This means (conservative, traditional and conventional clothing)—clothing that is faddish or has exceptionally bold patterns or colours attracts attention—unfortunately, away from you.

- **Gulf national (Men)**—should be dressed in the traditional Arabic (dishdasha) with the (Agal and ghutra). The dishdasha should be ironed and spotless. New is recommended.
- **Gulf national (Women)**—if you wear (Abaya) then it should be clean and ironed. If you do not wear an abaya I recommend a business suit. It is formal and very presentable again, ironed and spotless.

- **Other nationalities (Men)**—a business suit is recommended not shirt and tie. The colour of the suit should be conservative (pinstriped, dark blue, dark or light grey, dark green). Please do not wear any other colours they give the wrong impression. The suit should be ironed and spotless. Shirt should be white spotless and ironed. Conservative tie colour, nothing bright and colourful, and for goodness sake no pictures on the tie.

- **Other nationalities (Women)**—a business suit is recommended (if the colours are not bright and colourful there is no problem.) I do not recommend that ladies from the subcontinent like India, Pakistan and Sri Lanka wear saris or shalwar kameez. These clothes may look nice but they do not give a professional look. These clothes are good for the home, shopping and parties, but not recommended in the office and especially in an interview.

Note: Do not wear low-cut blouses, short skirts, tight clothes or clothing that appear "Sexy." Remember you are looking for a job and you do not wish to give the wrong impression about yourself.

- **Shoes and bags**—shoes must be polished and clean, in the case of ladies the bags should not be too bulky and disorganised, it is recommended that the colour of the bag matches the colour of the shoe.

Story: a client of mine who came to me after she was unable to get a job for more than six months, with my help she finally managed to get a job that she enjoys very much. She told me a story that once happened to her. That she was asked to come to an interview on a particular day, so she got dressed and just before she left home she made her son a sandwich. She did not know it, but she got some Ketchup on her white shirt. After reaching the location of the interview she saw the stain and cleaned it, but a small mark was left on the silk shirt. She informed me that even though 99% of her shirt was clean everyone's eye was on the small red spot on her shirt.

Remember the way you dress is the way you would like to be treated. If you dress shabbily, people will treat you that way. If you are smart and well dressed, you demand respect from people.

B. How to look

The way you look is very important let me handle each aspect separately.

- **Hair (Men)**—should be combed if you have a problem with your hair (bad hair day) please use a hairspray.

- **Hair (Women)**—same as men combed, for goodness sake please do not go to an interview looking like your head exploded, if you did not know it there is a great invention called hair band and hair pins.

- **Jewellery (Men)**—I am not against men wearing jewellery but do not wear any for the interview. I recommend only one ring, a wedding band or engagement ring nothing more. If you normally wear rings, take them off for the interview.

- **Jewellery (Women)**—I know that women love to wear Jewellery, but remember you are going to an interview and not a party or a fashion show. So please keep it to a bare minimum, and nothing too flashy.

C. Body odour (BO)

This is very important if you feel that you have BO, then please do use deodorant and perfume. There are few things we can control, and not controlling such a problem is a show of disrespect. If you feel that you have such a problem, please take care of it.

As you know the Middle East is a hot region, so in the summer months the temperatures goes up to 45+ Celsius. In such a situation, people start sweating, so by the time a job hunter enters the company he or she may be soaked in sweat. What do you do in such a situation?

- The first thing to do is go to the men's or women's restroom and start fixing what the weather spoiled.

- After you feel that you now look presentable, go and find a seat that is well cooled and start feeling fresh.

If you meet someone for the first time and that person looks so fresh, cool and relaxed. You would very much like to know the secret of that person. Suddenly, this complete stranger is now a person in position of a great secret. Also, if you look fresh you do not give a message to the interviewer that you are nervous. Stay cool and look fresh.

D. Makeup

Many women put on too much makeup for the interview. Remember keep the makeup to a minimum and do not overdo it. Remember you would like to work in this organisation, and you do not want to look like you are on the way to an evening party.

E. Perfume

Using perfume is fine but some people have a habit of taking a shower in perfume or that is how it appears, when they walk into a room the entire room smells of the perfume, they have showered in.

The following is the responses that were received when the survey was conducted regarding the dress code for interviews:

91% The job hunter should be well dressed

8% The job hunter should be presentable

1% Dress is not important

4. Arriving on time for the interview

Arriving on time for the interview is very important. If the interview is supposed to start at 11:00 a.m., then you had better be there at 10:50 a.m. this will give you a chance to get ready for the interview. Remember the restroom. It does not look good that you arrive late and keep the interviewer waiting for you.

Too much traffic or parking problems is not an excuse. You should have anticipated this. If you cannot manage your time, how can you manage the organisations work. So always be ahead of time this will demonstrate that you have excellent time management skills, even though you did not put this skill in your CV.

5. Waiting room strategies

• Ask the receptionist for the name of the interviewer (if you do not already know it)

• Skim through any company literature provided in the waiting room (to add new insights to your knowledge of the organisation—particularly product or service information)

• Do your relaxation exercises

6. What not to do during an interview

There are many things that people do during an interview that directly affects their chances of getting the job. Let me list these items to make things simpler:

- **Smoking**—you should never under any circumstance smoke during an interview. Even if the interviewer is smoking you should not.

- **Laughing**—if you hear a joke or something funny smiling is good but not laughing out aloud. You may feel the erg to laugh, but this is not recommended. You must always be composed and in control of yourself.

- **Fidgeting**—fidgeting is considered as a sign of nervousness and you do not wish to appear nervous. Many people start playing with a piece of paper or pencil, some people start shaking their legs. If you see yourself doing this stop it at once.

- **Looking at the window**—during an interview some people have a bad habit of looking outside the window. Remember you are sitting for an interview and not to look at the view. Also, if a room does not have a window some people have a habit of looking at the items in the room or ceiling. I fail to understand why! Is there any writing on the walls or on the ceiling that will help you answer the question the interviewer has asked you?

- **Eye contact**—many people do this strange thing. When an interviewer is talking to them, they tend to look at the floor and not focus on the interviewer. This gives the interviewer the wrong impression about you, that either you are nervous or trying to hide something from him or her. Remember: when you are spoken to look at the interviewer directly in the eye and respond to his or her questions looking at him or her in the eye. Ask yourself this question when talking to your friends or family members, do you look them in the eye or not? If yes, then do the same in the interview. This is a skill that needs to be developed especially by those people who are shy.

- **Stop playing with your face**—Some people have a habit of playing with their face. Putting their hands on their mouths or rubbing their ears. Why? Your hands should be down either on the table or on the armrest of the chair and try to restrict the movements of your hands.

- **Stop reading what is on the interviewer's table**—some people have a habit of reading the documents that are on the interviewer's table. Stop that! Also stop trying to read the interviewer's written comments about you.

- **Do not talk too much**—some people like to talk and when asked a question they will go on and on talking. Remember that you should only answer the question, do not go overboard by giving your life story. Keep to the topic at hand and nothing more.

- **Listen then talk**—people tend to interrupt the interviewer when he or she is talking. Stop listen to the question and when the interviewer has stopped talking then begin to respond.

- **Drinks**—if the interviewer asks you if you would like to have anything to drink (tea, coffee, cold drink, etc.), decline the offer, but if you feel that you have a dry throat then just ask for a glass of water. Nothing more. I remember a gentleman who came in for an interview and was asked by the HR Director if he would like to have anything to drink? Yes, was the answer. I would like a café latte with vanilla please. We were five panel members we just started looking at each other, needless to say he did not get the JOB.

- **Be polite**—always say please and thank you, never ever use adult or colourful language during an interview. I remember during an interview a gentleman was using The F word in every sentence, as it was quite normal for him but not the language used in the organisation.

7. What should you do during an interview

We have covered all the things you should not do, now let us discuss the things that you should do during an interview.

- **Greeting**—Greet the interviewer with eye contact and a relaxed smile. Look into the interviewer's eyes as you are greeted, not at the floor or elsewhere.

- **Shaking Hands**—Be ready to shake hands, but let the interviewer take the lead. If the interviewer does not extend a hand, do not initiate the handshake. It is common to shake hands in business. But if the interviewer does not take the initiative, there is a reason. Perhaps the interviewer feels uncomfortable with physical contact. There could be a religious reason if the interviewer is a woman. Whatever the reason, it simply is safer to take the cue from the interviewer.

When shaking hands, you must use a firm grip. Not like some people who are very stingy they give you some fingers to shake hands with. You may think that it seems ridiculous for an interviewer to attach any significance to how you shake hands; nevertheless, it does make an impact. Weak handshakes are often interpreted as revealing lack of self-confidence

- **Interviewer's Name**—Use the interviewer's name when greeting him or her. Unless the interviewer invites you to use his or her first name, it is best to remain formal and respectful by using Mr. or Ms. this can be a little tricky with women interviewers. It is often difficult to know whether to use Ms. or Mrs. One easy way to solve the dilemma is to start by introducing yourself and then listening very carefully to how the interviewer presents her name. It typically will go like this:

  — **"Good morning, I am Ebrahim Mohammed."**

  — **"Good morning, Ebrahim, I am Mrs. Stevens or I am Aisha Abdulla."**

  Remember the name and use it during the interview.

- **Walk Erect**—Remember that you must walk erect and with some vigour. I have seen applicants create a negative first impression – even before they have uttered a word. They entered the interview room slouching or shuffling, as though they had just gotten out of bed and were still half asleep.

- **Smile**—Smiling is good during an interview, not too much, but at the right time. Some people appear to be so serious, that the interviewer feels uncomfortable talking to them.

- **Take a Seat**—Sit down but not before the interviewer sits down or offers you a chair. As you are about to sit down, consider adjusting the chair so that you do not have to face the interviewer directly, eyeball to eyeball. This act shows confidence and is likely to be more comfortable. It also allows you to demonstrate interest, and attentiveness as, during the interview, you will turn your head and shoulders to face the interviewer.

  Sit comfortably, as far back in the chair as possible. Persons who sit on the front edge often appear tense. Sitting back will also help you feel more relaxed.

- **Copy of Resume**—It is very important to take a copy of your updated CV or resume to the interview. What may happen is that some months may have passed since you had sent your resume to the prospect employer and the date of the interview. And you may have updated your resume in those months.

- **Breath Mints**—This is a matter of being safe rather than sorry. Not only is there the obvious problem of the odour of food, but very often anxiety can result in bad breath. Popping a few mints in your mouth before the interview can eliminate one problem that might create a poor initial impression; you will have one less thing to worry about.

- **Mobile Phone**—Remember to turn your mobile phone off during the interview. It does not look good that you are in an interview and the mobile phone starts ringing. "Murphy's law states—if something has to go wrong it will go wrong." So please switch-off your mobile phone.

Note: If the interviews take place over more than one day, wear a different outfit each day. If for some reason, wearing a different suit or dress each day is not feasible, then at least put on a fresh shirt and different tie; women can benefit from wearing a fresh blouse and different accessories.

Remember: A Resumes is a doorway to the interview and the interview is doorway to getting that dream job.

Sources of Information

- Drake, John D. 1997. *"The Perfect Interview" How to Get the Job You Really Want*, 2nd ed. Amacom American Management Association, New York
- Saad E. Abbas 2007. *"How to Get the Right Job"* Department of Economic Development, Dubai.

2   How to Respond to Interview Questions

Anyone who has been interviewed for a job has probably learned that it is difficult to answer certain questions without conveying something negative. One such classic question is, "What are some of your shortcomings (weaknesses)?" it is important to anticipate these "sticky questions" and to rehearse how you will respond to them.

The Two Basic Types of Tough Questions

There are two basic kinds of questions that present problems for most job seekers. One group consists of questions that require you to talk about or evaluate yourself. An example of such a question is "What is there about you that would make you an effective supervisor?"

The second type of tough question requests the application to solve a problem—real or hypothetical. An example of this line of questioning is, "What do you think is the ideal way to minimise conflicts between sales and manufacturing departments?" sometimes these questions are phrased in hypothetical terms, such as, "Suppose one of your best subordinates indicates that he wants to leave the company. How would you handle such a situation?"

Twelve of the Toughest Questions

The most frequently asked "sticky questions" are described next, along with suggestions about how to prepare for them. Exactly how you answer them will depend on your background and personality. However, it should be fairly easy to adapt these principles to your own situation.

1. Tell me about yourself?

This is the granddaddy of all self-report questions. For most job applicants, it is also the most difficult one to respond to. If you have not prepared yourself and rehearsed an answer to this question, it is likely that you will come across in an unimpressive way.

For most interviewers, what you say in response to this question is not as important as how you handle it. Most frequently people tend to say too much. Interviewees usually give too much detail—they bore the interviewer, start talking about irrelevant things or reveal information about themselves that is better left unsaid.

This is an effective strategy for answering the "Tell me about yourself" question. It is called three steps and a bridge. It covers four areas:

1. Y our early background (where you were brought up)
2. Your education
3. Your work experiences
4. A bridging statement such as, "and that background leads me here today to this assignment."

The idea is to touch briefly on each of the first three areas and single out a few significant achievements. You then follow this summary by a bridging phase.

Following is an example of how you might use the three-steps-and-a-bridge method:

"I was brought up in Dubai. Both my parents were schoolteachers, so the idea of getting a good education was instilled in me early on.

In secondary school, I was quite good at math. My teachers and my parents thought that engineering would be a natural for me. I also liked the science courses, so I also thought that some sort of career in technology would be good.

After graduation, I was accepted at ABC University and got a B.S. in mechanical engineering. While there I was an officer in a social fraternity and was elected president of the senior class. I also did quite well academically, making the Dean's list seven out of eight semesters.

After ABC University, I took up a job with "Blue Chemical Company," starting in their management training program. After two years, I was assigned to a large plant in Jebel Ali Free Zone, and soon found myself involved in a major production control problem for which I was able to develop a solution—a computerised program. Soon after, I was moved up to supervisory position. I found that I enjoyed managing as much as engineering and I was very effective as a department head.

The management experience led me to pursue an MBA in the evenings. Then, two years later, I was contacted by a head-hunter who told me of a unique opportunity at "Black and Grey Corporation." They wanted somebody with high-tech production experience and computer know-how. The job attracted me because it gave me a chance to advance in management and work on the development of new equipment.

I have been with Black and Grey Corporation for three years as assistant manager of technical development, and it is [THE BRIDGE] (this combination of engineering experience, computer know-how, and management that leads me here today to the position we are discussing.)"

In every instance, you will find that an answer of this sort, that takes only two minutes, makes a positive impression. Because this is such a common and yet crucial question, it would be well worthwhile to shape your answer before your next interview.

There is one problem that some job seekers may face with this question. An interviewer may ask you to (**Talk about yourself reverse chronologically?**) So, what you will have to do in this case is start from your current job and work backwards. The good news is that this is very rare, in my experience, I have seen it used once and that was 20 years ago.

2.   What are your strengths?

This question should be looked at as a welcome gift. It provides a wonderful opportunity to tell the interviewer about some specific and important attributes that you possess.

In preparing your answers to this question, mention at least four or five strengths. This enables you to present a wide range of assets and to project a good level of self-confidence. If you present fewer than four, it does not say much about your self-image.

Factors that account for success at work

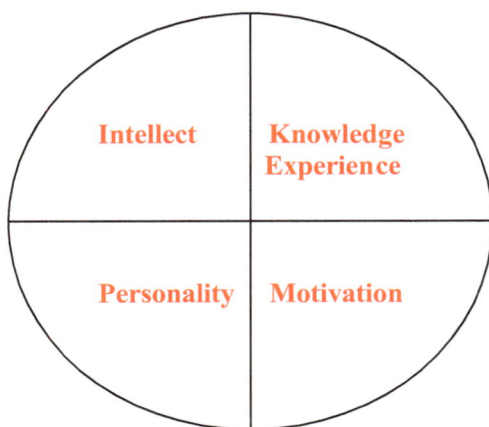

Intellect | Knowledge Experience

Personality | Motivation

A. **Intellect**. This factor has nothing to do with knowledge; it relates to capabilities in two dimensions—natural ability (quantitative, verbal, mechanical and artistic) and how you usually process your thoughts (think quickly on your feet, think in a logical deductive manner). Here are four examples:

- **One thing about me is that I believe I am bright. I learn very fast and can usually pick up on what must be done in a very short time.**
- **I have good quantitative skills—I find it very easy to work with numbers.**
- **I am usually quite decisive because I can think quickly on my feet.**
- **I seem to have good conceptual ability. I usually look at problems from a broad perspective.**

B. **Knowledge and Experience.** There is no mystery about this factor. It is just what it sounds like—educational or work achievements that are pertinent to the job for which you are applying. Here are a few examples:

- **My ten years of sales experience with XYZ Company should enable me to develop an effective key accounts campaign.**
- **The training I have had in computer sciences should enable me to step in and be productive from day one.**

Note: See how it is helpful to mention the know-how or experience and then relate that to what it could positively mean for the company.

C. **Personality.** This factor has to do with your behavioural characteristics (how you interact with others) and your temperament (how you typically behave). Here are some examples:

- **I seem to have an ability to relate to people at all levels in the company. I am interested in others and I think they sense that.**
- **Another strength I have is that I do not get discouraged easily. If I run into an obstacle, I am likely to persist until I find some way around it.**

D. **Motivation.** This factor has to do with your interests (activities you enjoy doing), your drive and your energy level. Here are some examples:

- **I am quite extroverted (demonstrative). While I am good at technical problem solving, I really enjoy working with others. I find supervising stimulating and challenging.**
- **I like to pay a lot of attention to fine points. I do not just skip through a job; I exercise a lot of care and, as a result, I am accurate.**
- **I have always been a self-starter. I guess I have a lot of drive because I get tremendous satisfaction out of seeing a goal accomplished.**
- **I have a high energy level. I can work long hours without getting tired.**

To make the most out of this question, it is helpful to write out your assets. Try to develop six or even seven, at least one for each of the four factors.

3.   What are your major weaknesses or limitations?

First of all, you should recognise that this question is often phrased in more subtle ways, usually in an effort to make the question appear less threatening to the applicant. Some common ways in which it is stated are

- **What are some areas in which you can improve?**
- **How have you grown over the past few years?**
- **Where do you see yourself needing to grow in the near future?**

Second, it is not a good strategy to attempt to avoid mentioning shortcomings. Unless you are extremely sure of yourself, ducking the shortcomings issue will come across as being defensive, a sign of weakness. On the other hand, you do not have to condemn yourself either. My recommendation is to mention one or two limitations and state them in such a way that they are not damaging to you.

You may face a problem if the interviewer asks you to list five weaknesses or limitations. In this case list, only three and say I do not think I have any more weaknesses. There are two basic techniques for responding to this question and they are

- Mention weaknesses that mirror your assets.
- Mention weaknesses that are easily remedied.

Let us begin with the "mirror concept" of presenting your weaknesses.

Many job seekers find this question difficult or awkward to deal with. Actually, it can be comfortable to answer, once a certain principle is understood: your weaknesses are almost always over extensions of your strengths. For instance, if you are action-oriented, the positive side is that you are probably decisive, can juggle many projects at once, and get much accomplished in a short period of time. However, when you overplay your strength, you are likely to be criticised for being impatient, not paying enough attention to detail, and not being well organised. When you formulate an answer to the weaknesses question, simply select one of your strengths and admit that sometimes, because of the strength, a particular weakness is evident. Here are two examples:

- **I tend to look at problems from a "big picture" point of view, and sometimes I do not pay enough attention to the details.**
- **I am a high-energy person and push myself pretty hard. I have to be careful sometimes not to move ahead before my staff are ready.**

This strategy is an ideal way to talk about weaknesses. First of all, it is honest. It will ring true along with the positive things you have said about yourself. Second, when you respond by revealing weaknesses that are an overplay of your strengths, your openness conveys self-assurance. That behaviour, in its own right, creates a favourable impression on most interviews. You are not likely to be evaluated as being defensive.

The second suggestion for responding to the weaknesses question is to mention something that is easily remedied. The simplest way to do this is to offer an example and then state what you intend to do about it. Example:

- **I would like to take some formal courses in supervision. So far, I have only had my job experiences along with some reading on my own.**
- **I would like to strengthen my knowledge of computer applications in sales**

- I could probably improve my public speaking skills—I would like to take a Toastmasters or Dale Carnegie course.
- I would like to broaden my managerial skills. I plan to start working on my MBA by taking evening courses.

4.   What are your financial requirements?

The most important thing is not to say, "It is not that important to me—opportunity is my primary concern." Of course, opportunity is a big element in your employment decisions, but compensation is also very important. Would you accept a new job for 20% less then what you are making now? Money is very important not only for how it allows you to live but for what it says about the importance of the job. The more you are paid the higher you are on the corporate ladder. The point is that money is usually an important issue, and as a job seeker, you are not likely to come across as convincing if you duck the question.

In considering how to answer the money question, two issues need to be weighed:

- How much do you want?
- How much will they pay?

It is very important to remember that no one can recommend the right salary for you, there is a way to formulate an answer to this question. You must ask yourself "What is the minimum amount I will accept?" this amount should be an amount below which you will not consider the job. This amount will permit you to live on the borderline of the lifestyle you want. Write this amount down.

Now you must ask yourself another question, "How much do I really want?" Write this amount down.

Now that you have decided upon the two amounts, you have a working range, an "acceptance zone" in which to discuss salary.

Now we came to the next part and that is how much is the organisation willing to pay? If you already know this (because of an advertised salary or other source), and assuming the stated salary falls into your acceptance zone, you can mention a somewhat higher salary than is being offered. It is always easier to back down to the posted amount than to try to go up, once you have stated a desired salary.

If you do not know the salary the organisation has in mind, try to find out the expected amount before you mention your amount. Here you will find a way of getting at that number:

When the interviewer asks you about your salary requirements, you can respond by asking a question of your own:

"I would like to answer that question, but would you mind sharing with me the salary grade range for this job?"

If the interviewer states the range, it is usually prudent to select a figure that is halfway between the midpoint and the top of the salary range. You may have to back down to the midpoint, but if you mention a number below that amount, you have given away any negotiating strength.

If the interviewer is unwilling to talk about the grade range or the salary amount, one option is to mention an amount equal to your current salary plus 15%. The main thing to understand is the amount of compensation you ask for really depends on how much you believe you are worth. There are times when it may be quite appropriate to ask for two or three times your current salary. The determining factor is how much your prospective employer believes you are worth.

You must remember that answering the how much question is not looking for an answer or seeming embarrassed about what to say. Before you go to the interview, you should know your acceptance zone and state your financial desires firmly and confidently.

5. Why [are you leaving/did you leave] your present job?

When an interviewer asks this question, he or she is looking to discover if you were terminated, or eased out, or quit because things were not going well for you on the job. Very specifically, the interviewer is concerned about your ability to get along with people. Remember that the interviewer will be listening very carefully to your wording, looking to pick up any negative attitudes towards your co-workers or bosses.

Let us look at some reasons for leaving a job. When you are asked why you left or would like to leave a job, remember it is not what you say but how you say it that is important. There should be no hint of defensiveness. Make your answer brief and matter of fact. For instance:

Situation: Fired Because of a Major Downsizing

- [Bad Answer] As you know, the company has been experiencing difficulty in the past several years, and they have gradually had to reduce staff. But last month, things really got serious and ...
- [Good Answer] **Last month, the company had a major downsizing, and like most of the technical staff, I got caught in it.**

As you can see both statements say the same thing, with one exception the first statement gives a negative picture about the company. Remember that no matter how shabbily the company you worked for treated you. You must never talk about that company in a negative way. The reason for this is that if you talk about your last company in a bad light, you will talk negatively about the company, wherein you are applying for if you are not happy in the job.

If you left your last job because you were fired remember to say the truth, trying to avoid what actually happened will not help. When you say you were fired, it is important not to say anything negative about the cause of termination like low motivation or inability to work effectively with others. Look at the example below:

Situation: Fired because of a conflict with boss

- [Bad Answer] **My boss and I did not get along that well**
- [Good Answer] **To be perfectly frank with you, I got fired. My boss and I had completely different management styles. We both respected each other, so over the years we had more or less agreed to disagree. But eventually he wanted more things done his way than I was willing to do.**

Situation: Performance was not what the boss wanted

- [Bad Answer] **Even though I was doing everything the boss wanted, I just could not do enough to please my boss.**
- The job really did not let me capitalise on my best talents. I have good ability to supervise and motivate others, but I was mostly tied up with backroom technical assignments.

If you are still working and you are asked why would you like to leave your current job? The answer is very simple just say (better prospects, looking for a change in my career, I am looking for a job that is closer to my family, other) let your response match your situation.

Note: Never say anything negative.

6. What are your career goals for the next five years?

When the interviewer asks this type of question, the interviewer is looking for two things:

Your drive and ambition

Most people do not have five-year plans, so if you are uncertain about your future, it is important to give a general desire for continued growth. If you say that you have no career goals, the interviewer will interpret that response negatively.

- [Bad Answer] **I do not have any particular goals for the next five years. I like to look at opportunities as they come.**

- [Good Answer] **I like to have the feeling that I am continually growing, so in the next five years I want to increase my competence in …**

On the other hand, being too ambitious is also very risky.

- [Poor Answer] **My goal is to become a top executive in this company. I expect that with my drive I will move ahead very rapidly.**

The part about becoming a "top executive" is fine, but once you add the words "very rapidly" you sound like someone whose ambition overrides everything else. Some interviewers may feel threatened by such a comment.

In today's "flat" organisations, rapid advancement is not typical. It is best to make a balance: show the desire for progress and growth but be realistic considering the job level and the organisation.

If you have specific career objectives, it is usually helpful to state them. The risk is that they might be incompatible with the company's view or the opportunities available. If you know the organisation and you have a good idea about company's expectations and also then you can state, the following:

- **Within the next two years I would like to advance to the level of sales supervisor so that at the end of four or five years I would be ready for promotion to area sales manager.**

If your expectations for advancement match what the company can offer.
When you are not sure about the match between your goals and those of the organisation, it is prudent to bring your goals down a bit until you can learn more about future possibilities in the company. You may state the following:

*   **Within the next five years I want to expand my professional selling skills and advance to sales management—but I would need to know a little more about your organisation to tell you exactly what level or when.**

7. What kind of a position are you looking for?

This question is much like "Tell me about yourself," this can be difficult to respond to because it is easy to say too much or the wrong thing. From the interviewer's standpoint what you want may be different from the job the company is trying to fill. The company may be looking for a secretary; you are seeking a position as office manager. The company is looking for someone who is willing to travel, and you would like a more regular job with regular hours.

When you answer this question try to use it as an opportunity to highlight your strengths. It is safer, to avoid using specific job titles unless you have applied for a specific position. Here are some examples:

*   **I am looking for a job where I can apply my skills with people** [mention here those specific skills or activities you enjoy].
*   **I am looking for a job in which I can use my good technical skills** [mention here what they are].
*   **I am looking for an opportunity that allows me to use my skills with** [things / machines / tools].

8. What accomplishment was the most significant in your last position?

This question gives you another excellent opportunity to sell yourself. But it requires some thought and preparation. A good interviewer will be trying to determine your true role in the accomplishment. Experience has taught them that job seekers often describe important projects in which they played a part but which they did not actually propose, create, design or manage.

The interviewer will be trying to determine if a consultant or someone else actually managed the project, for which the job seeker is trying to take credit.

The best answer to this question is that you will need to think of an achievement that was clearly "your baby" and that had a positive impact. It will also help if you can describe some obstacles that you overcame, or any resistance to the project. Here is an example:

- **Last year, even though the company reorganised, and I lost four salespeople, I was able through extensive "hands-on" training of the remaining sales force, to increase sales in my district by 30%.**

This is a very likely question if the job for which you are being interviewed is at a lower level of responsibility

9. Doesn't this job represent a step down from your last job?

Or less salary than your last job. The interviewer will be concerned that you are only taking this job as a steppingstone for a better job, and that you will leave as soon as something better comes along. As a job seeker you must convince the interviewer that if you get the job, you will be committed to the job. Here are two examples:

- **I like what I have learned about this job, and, as with every job I have taken, I will give it my best.**

In every job situation, I think employers worry about people leaving just as employees worry about getting terminated. I will do a good job for you and stay just as long as we both agree that this is what I should be doing.

10. How would you describe your management style?

Your response to this question can result in you looking bad, particularly if you seem hesitant in your response. After all, the interviewer expects that if you supervise others in a particular management style, you should be able to talk about it easily. If you are unable to talk about your management style that will cast some doubt on your ability and experience as a manager.

This question can sometimes be difficult if you are not sure of the prevailing style in the interviewer's organisation. However, if you have done your homework, while researching the company you may have come across some information on the management style of the organisation.

There are three basic ways to answer this question, depending on how hungry you are for the position.

A. **Be brutally honest**. If you have a definite way of managing and you can spell it out clearly and confidently, that is great. The upside is that you will sound as if you know what you are doing and have been successful with your approach. The downside is that what you say may be incompatible with the way the organisation works. But the risk is likely to be fairly minimal unless your management style is highly unusual example. (I make all the decisions.)

B. **Key your style to that of the organisation**. Some companies have a definite personality that translates into a management pattern. These organisations are often proud of their management style and clearly look for people who would fit into that style. This is an example response:

- **I am inclined to be demanding of my staff, but participative. I spell out to them what I expect, listen carefully to their reactions and, once we agree, I give them lots of hope. They know I am there if they have a serious problem, but they also know I expect the results we agreed on, at the time we agreed on.**

C. **Play it safe**. If you are uncertain of the company's corporate style, you can present a very acceptable answer by mentioning one of several management approaches that are currently seen as effective. Pick one that comes close to describing your actual behaviour. Here are a few examples:

- **I like to operate in a participative way. Whenever possible I get commitment from my staff by involving them in the planning and objective setting.**

- **I have a lot of respect for my staff. I usually give them plenty of hope but clearly hold them accountable. I like to have time to work on ways to improve the bottom line, so I delegate quite freely.**

11. How would you approach this job?

"Suppose you came on board tomorrow, what is the first thing you would do?" Or, "What actions would you take during your first week [or month] on the job?" These are frequently asked variations of the same basic question.

Interviewers often use these questions when the job you are applying for involves a "sticky" or sensitive situation, example, you may be applying for a managerial position in a department that has recently been downsized; morale is low and everyone is concerned that the axe may fall soon again. The interviewer wants to see how you are likely to manage the situation and what will be the impact of your actions on the department staff.

You may think this is unfair. How can I answer a question about what I would do if I do not know exactly what is going on? That is why this question is very risky. To minimise the danger, you do not answer immediately; you try to gain more information about the job by asking a question of your own. You can attempt to gain a sense of what the interviewer is looking for.

You might say, for instance, "I would be happy to answer that question, but it would help if I had a better understanding of exactly what the current situation is like. Can you fill me in a bit?"

Responding with a question rather than giving a direct answer will be inappropriate if the job setting has already been discussed or the situation is obvious. In this case, a few general principles can help you formulate an acceptable answer:

A. **Recognise that, once you are on the job, you will need to survey the new world you have stepped into**. Say that you will initially spend time gathering information (from subordinates, sales staff, boss, whoever) in order to learn "first-hand" what needs to be done.

B. **Try to visualise yourself in the assignment**. What do you think the major issues to be dealt with are? You can say, "I imagine that one issue would be..." and look to the interviewer for signs of confirmation or rejection. The interviewer's body language may provide a clue as to whether or not you are on the right track.

C. **Do not try to explain how you would solve a major problem**. Try to state a few first steps you would take to start your work. Having said this, I realise that the question can still be a killer if you say the wrong thing. The best thing to do is to rely on your past experience and state the actions and decisions that have worked for you in the past.

12.   Please give me a 360-degree feedback from (supervisors, colleagues and subordinates)?

This is a very new question that has been added to the interview questions list in the past few years. When you first look at this question, it appears to be very complicated, but it is not. The response to this question should be broken down into three parts.

- **Part One. What would your Superior (Boss) say about you?** Remember every year your superior does your appraisal, what does he normally say about your strong points. Example (Friendly, hardworking, helps colleagues and subordinates completes assignments, works well under pressure, completes tasks before deadline, good time management skills, etc.)

- **Part Two. What would your Colleagues say about you?** Remember when talking in the corridors with other managers what praises have, they given you. Example (very frank, meets you with a smile, has a good and reliable network, helpful, if consulted regarding a problem situation always comes to you with a usable solution, very good communicator, excellent negotiator, etc.)

- **Part Three. What would your Subordinates (Staff) say about you?** Remember when you used to do your staff's appraisals, did any of them thank you? Why? Example: (very supportive of staff, consults staff before setting targets, supports staff training, has an open door policy, if staff achieves target he gives that member of the staff support for advancement, very strict with work, good staff motivator, keeps the office environment friendly and supportive, etc.)

One of the latest questions I have heard during an interview was this: list 3 words that describe you? You must find there words that best describe your abilities. It is advisable not to copy from someone else as your abilities are not the same as other people. Example responses are "I would describe myself as organized, patient and helpful" or any of the following or more Passionate, Enthusiastic, Innovative, Creative, Driven, Communicative, Approachable, Motivator, Team Player, Reliable etc.

Sources of Information

- Drake, John D. 1997. *"The Perfect Interview" How to Get the Job You Really Want*, 2nd ed. Amacom American Management Association, New York.
- Saad E. Abbas 2007. *"How to Get the Right Job"* Department of Economic Development, Dubai.

3 What are the Different Types of Interviews?

What Interviewers Are Looking For?

Basically, interviewers are looking for the answers to two questions:

- Can you do the Job?
- Are you our kind of person?

The first issue, "Can you do the Job?" is a challenge for all job seekers because the interviewer is concerned that you may not do what you say you can do. Your basic task, during the interview, is to help the interviewer see what you do, and how you do it, and that you will be an asset to the organisation.

The interviewer is usually trying to find out what is not good about you. **Are you shocked**? Look at it this way. The interviewer would not be talking with you unless you already had met most of the organisation's requirements for the job. After the interviewer screened your Resume he or she has concluded that you have the qualifications for the job. But experience has also taught the interviewer that people are not all that they appear to be. Work experience and educational background can be distorted to look better than is the actual case. Also, it is not just what experience or knowledge you have. The interviewer is more interested in how you accomplished your achievements. The interviewer wants to find out if your working style will interfere with your ability to perform effectively or you are compatible with how the company operates.

The second issue, "Are you our kind of person?" or "will you fit in?" the best way to take care of this question is to just sell yourself.

It is very important for the interviewer to like you as a person. Interviewers are most often willing to accept a less qualified candidate (in terms of knowledge or experience) just because they feel more comfortable with them or they may feel that this candidate will fit better into the working environment of the organisation.

I recommend that during an interview, you should be relaxed and be yourself, this will help gain acceptance from interviewers. If you make an effort at role playing or consciously trying to impress the interviewer by showing characteristics that are not truly yours, this usually will backfire. You just will not give the interviewer the right message, by trying to be someone else.

Gate-keeping Interviews: And How to Manage Them

In your search for employment, you are likely to encounter five different kinds of interviews, depending on where the interview takes place and / or what stage you are in an organisation's hiring process. Three of these can be termed gatekeeper interviews—each is a gateway to further interviews in the hiring process. They are

- The human resource department
- The employment agency
- The executive search firm (head-hunters)

The two other basic types of interviews are the semi-final, occurring between the gate keeping and the final interview, that is where (to hire or not to hire that is the question!) decision is made.

1. The human resources interview:

As the name implies, this is an interview that takes place in the Personnel Department or Human Resource Department. You will not encounter it in every job-hunting situation, but it will almost always occur if you are applying for employment in a large organisation.

Whom will you encounter?

This interview will usually be conducted by an experienced interviewer. Most often the interviewer will be a woman. She will usually make an effort to put you at ease but at the same time will not hesitate to ask tough questions about your background.

What is the interviewer looking for?

The most important thing to remember about this interview is that it is a screening interview. The interviewer will try to determine if your background is all that your Resume says it is. Your primary job will be to get past this screen to the people who will actually make the hiring decision. You must understand that this interviewer has the power to reject you but does not have the power to hire you. So be very careful!

You must understand that the interviewer has problems confronting her. First, she usually has a large number of people to interview in a day, so she is pressured by time. Second, she must find a candidate that meets the job specifications.

How to make the best impression during the HR interview?

When you consider the time issue and the screening nature of the human resource interview, the approach you should adopt is very clear.

- Be prepared to present key factual data about your background.

- Make your comments brief rather than too long and complete. Remember the interviewer does not have a lot of time.

- Let the interviewer control the pace and discussion.

- Be concise and to the point, do not give too much information that can hurt you more than it can help you.

2.   The employment agency interview

It is very important to understand employment agencies operate on a commission basis. If they refer you to an organisation and you get hired, they get paid anywhere from 10 to 30 percent of your starting salary. They only get paid if you get hired and work out well. The more people they see and refer to prospective employers the more money they get paid. For this reason, the interviews are brief (thirty minutes or less).

Whom will you encounter?

Interviewers in most agencies are experienced; they have interviewed a large number of job seekers. Most interviewers are young and aggressive. Sometimes, if the job is a specialised one, you may encounter an experienced old-timer who knows his client's needs and who knows exactly what he wants to learn about you.

What is the interviewer looking for?

Interviewers are looking for any skills or experiences that are marketable. Unlike a human resources interviewer, the agency interviewer hopes you can qualify for job openings he knows about (or hopes to learn about). He is trying to fit you into a job rather than screen you out.

How to make a good impression during your employment agency interviews?

- Be prepared to discuss your technical qualifications in a few words.

- Do not be surprised if the interviewer is intimidating (remember time pressure, they are hopping that you are good enough so that they can forward your Resume to their client. They want you as much as you need them)

- Be ready to take charge of the interview if the interviewer says. (I am sorry, but we do not have anything right now that matches your qualifications. but you have a good track record, and we will keep your Resume in our active files.) The interviewer may have overlooked some skills or experience in you Resume. It is now up to you to make certain they are seen. You can say something like this. (Before you end this interview, I was wondering if you realise that in my last job at ABC Bank, I made over one hundred commercial loans.) I supervised eight tellers and two assistant managers. I really know the banking business and how to go out and get new customers. In fact, in the two years I was there, I increased deposits by over one million.

3. Executive recruiter interview

Working with executive recruiters is complicated. There are so many possible points of contact and possible agendas. Executive recruiters are very different from employment agencies. Executive recruiters are hired by their clients to find candidates, and they are paid whether they fulfil the search or not.

In this section, I will discuss how to manage two different interview situations—the first, if you have initiated the interview; the second, if the recruiter has called you.

Whom will you encounter?

The interviewers you meet are likely to be experienced, competent and polished. A high proportion will be men; very often they will have been successful executives who formerly worked in the corporate world.

What is the interviewer looking for?

- The self-initiated interview:

- Remember, the interview is likely to be short.

- You have to make a good impression (you must talk about three points).
  - You have valuable experience.
  - You have a good track record.
  - You have the characteristics of a successful executive.

- The recruiter-initiated interview:
  It is very important that you effectively sell yourself. You must show that you look the part, you must communicate well, dress the part, and you must be socially accomplished. If you lack these skills, the recruiter will not spend much time with your accomplishments.

  Remember that in this case you are a buyer and the interviewer is after you. If you appear either too eager or too passive, the effect will not be good. The best thing to find out is what the interviewer has to offer is of any interest to you. There are two factors that will affect your interest:

- Does the interviewer really have a position for which he is conducting a real search?

- Is the position a good career opportunity for you?

The best way to become a buyer is to approach the interview with one thing in mind. Whether what is being offered is worth your time. The best way to do this is to ask questions. You may have some knowledge about the job from phone conversations here is your chance to get more information.

Here are some questions you can ask:

- Just so I can pace myself, how much time do we have?

- Do you want me to start by talking about myself, or can we start by talking about the position? I have a few questions I would like to ask you (be prepared with questions for example);

- What is the exact job title?

- To whom will I report?

- Could you tell me about the location?

- How many subordinates will report to me?
- What can you tell me about the compensation?

After you know that you are the finalist for this job, now you must ask for the company's name, explaining that you want to prepare for your meeting with the client.

The Semi-final and Final Interviews: How to Manage Them

Once you have gone past the gate keeping interview, one of two things will happen. One, you may be referred to someone who will interview you to make the final hire or / not to hire decision, or two, you will have a series of interviews with a variety of interviewers, since these two interview situations are different, I will discuss them separately.

4. Beauty parade interviews

Each of these interviews is likely to be for half an hour to one-hour duration. In a typical day, you may have as many as six to seven such interviews. The beauty parade interview is the semi-final interview; the reason for these interviews is to get a consensus approval from these different department heads, before you meet the final interviewer. After interviews are finished, they will compare their assessments of you and decide whether to make you an offer or pass you on to the decision-maker.

Whom will you encounter?

The interviewers in the beauty parade may include people who will be your superiors or peers in the department where you will be working, as well as key managers in areas with which your department will interact.

Most of these people who will interview you are largely untrained in interview skills. Also, they do not like the intrusion of the interview into their busy workday, especially if you will not be a member of their department. So be very careful what you say.

What beauty parade interviewers are looking for?

It is not easy to say what interviewers are after. You may be confronted with as many different approaches as there are interviewers. As a major rule beauty parade, interviewers are interested in two things:

- Can you do the job?
- Can I get along with this person?

How to make the best impact during the beauty parade

The best thing to do is to make sure you do not say anything that will threaten or alienate your interviewers. Be careful not to talk about changes you will make once you come on board. Instead talk about an interest in being helpful to each interviewer and his department. You will need to convey two things:

- That you are a good person, likable and enjoyable to work with.
- You know your stuff. You could be helpful. If you do not pass in either of these two areas, you will never get to the final, decision-making interview.

5. The final interview

This is the big interview with the person with the big corner office, this individual will make the hire or / not to hire decision. If you are hired, this person will be your immediate superior (your boss or your boss's boss).

What the final interviewer is looking for?

Let us begin with what the interviewer is not looking for. The final interviewer is not looking for an in-depth discussion about your technical skills. He will assume that other staff members have already explored your technical background in sufficient depth. He is looking for three things:

- How will you fit in? How will you mesh with the team? If his judgement is positive, then his evaluation of your potential for advancement may become the next key issue.
- Another area of focus for final interviewers concerns any problems that surfaced during earlier interviews (human resources or beauty parade). Earlier evaluations will have been forwarded to this interviewer, and he will want to check out some points for himself – particularly any areas that have raised question marks or doubts in the minds of previous interviewers.

- Finally, there is the "chemistry" issue. Do you think and act in ways that are compatible with this manager's personality?

How to make the best impact during the final interview?

Avoid volunteering extensive information about what you have done or how you have done it. If questions about knowledge or experience arise, you will respond to them. But answer each question as concisely as possible. In most instances, you should focus on significant accomplishments, rather than on details about how they were achieved.

Remember, the final interviewer's primary concern is not likely to be your technical competence.

It is very important that you speak positively about the organisation and the people you have met. You may be asked such questions as

- What are some of your reactions to what you have seen thus far?
- How did our team strike you?
- You will be working for Yousuf Mohammed. How did that interview go?

You should make direct clear statements about how impressed you were with the team you met. Do not forget that these are "his people"; it is quite likely that he selected them. Use the following example:

- **I was really impressed with how openly they spoke about their department problems and how Khalid, Abdulla and Maryam pitch in and help each other.**

Sometimes, as you proceed through the beauty parade, an interviewer may impress you as out of place or incompetent compared with the others you met. If the final interviewer asks about your reactions to the people you met, you are then faced with a dilemma, on the one hand you should be positive about what you observed; on the other hand, there is the issue of your credibility. You do not want to be judged as naïve or an idiot. You should be honest about your observations. Use the following example:

INTERVIEWER: What do you think of the people you have met so far?

APPLICANT: I was very much impressed by all the staff everyone seemed highly committed and excited about the future of the firm. The only one who seemed to view things a little differently was Abdul Kareem Jasim.

Non-traditional Interviews: How to Manage Them

Imagine arriving for what you expect will be a one-on-one interview only to find yourself in a conference room surrounded by five or six people, all of whom are interested in "dissecting" you. We will look at the following three interview situations and show you how to succeed:

6. The panel interview

What are Panel Interviews Like?

During a panel interview, you are questioned by three to six persons at the same time, this maybe an intimidating experience.

In most situations, the panellists will not be expert interviewers. The panel maybe composed of your prospective boss, perhaps your boss's boss, a human resources representative, a potential co-worker and a manager or two from closely aligned departments. For technical jobs, technical experts are often included.

The interview format is typically as follows:

A. Panel members introduce themselves.

B. A few "ice-breaking" comments are made.

C. You are asked a few broad, background questions such as:

- **Will you give us a brief description of your educational and work experiences?**
- **What are your responsibilities in your current [or last] job?**
- **What is there about this position that appeals to you?**

D. The remainder of the interview is likely to include one or both of the following questioning patterns:

- Each panellist asks his favourite questions so that the questioning is rarely in a logical order and covers a wide variety of topics.
- You are asked carefully planned, structured questions designed to evaluate your technical skills or personal qualities such as leadership potential, planning ability or conceptual skills.

E. You will then be asked if you have any questions

F. You will be provided with data about the job and the company

G. After about an hour, the conclusion will be signalled by a panellist—usually the HR representative saying something like, "Thank you so much for being with us today." Be alert for this cue because, at times, the ending may seem abrupt.

H. After your departure, the panellists will discuss your qualifications and make their ratings. In most cases, you will not receive immediate feedback as to the impression you have made.

How to succeed with panel interviews?

In a panel interview, you are asked to perform very much like an actor. You do not have the choice to get to know your interviewer like a one on one interview. Mostly, the questions will focus on breadth rather than depth.

If you are a good talker and comfortable in front of a group of people (audience), then you may find this very enjoyable. But if you are not comfortable in front of a group and you are a shy person, then I recommend that you practice at home with friends. Make sure you have eye contact with your interviewers.

Here are some suggestions for managing the perfect panel interview:

- Networking find out in advance all you can about the company and the company plans.

- Learn about the company goals and management style.

- When you are first introduced to each panel member, ask each member for his or her business card (keep the cards in front of you to mirror where each one is seated, so that you know the name of the interviewer who talking to you).

- You must know exactly what is in your Resume. What information is on what page.

- Do not be afraid to ask questions or to be up front about what you observe during the interview.

- Maintain good eye contact with each of your interviewers

- Be positive when you respond to any question

7.   Behavioural interviews

What are They Like?

These interviews are usually conducted one-on-one. Try to visualise an interview in which you are consistently asked to describe how or why you performed certain tasks or made particular decisions; you will know what a behavioural interview is like. The typical questions are

- You said that you are "good with people." What is it that you do that enables you to work effectively with others?
- What was the most difficult challenge you had to face in your last job? What did you do to overcome it?

Behavioural interviewers want to learn how you function and what motivates you. Because most of the questions are open-ended and require you to describe actions or thoughts, behavioural interviews tend to be long often lasting over an hour.

How to succeed with behavioural interviews?

Good news! These interviews are ideal for techniques taught in this book. The open-ended questions will give you a chance to mention your best skills and achievements. But you can run into a problem if you try to bluff the interviewer. Remember these interviewers are very good and experienced in this field so be honest. Here are some problem areas.

INTERVIEWER: How were you able to succeed in that difficult situation?

YOU: I was able to get the others to cooperate and work as a team.

INTERVIEWER: I see, but what did you do specifically that enabled you to gain their cooperation?

So how do you get around such difficulties and avoid the potential pitfalls? There are ways:

A.   Do not be afraid to pause and think through your answer before responding.

B.   Have in mind an organised format for answering open-ended conversations. Organise your thoughts like this:

- Briefly describe a situation or task.
- Explain the action or steps you took
- Describe the results of your action

Here is an example of this structure being used during a behavioural interview:

INTERVIEWER: Describe a time you decided to try a different approach to handling a customer problem. What happened?

APPLICANT: (Situation) An angry customer had been shouting at me for about ten minutes. Even though I had been sympathetic and was listing, nothing I could say seemed to calm her down. (Action) I know I had to try something different, so, instead of talking about our position, I imitated her feelings instead. I said, "You really seem upset and angry about what happened." (Results) What occurred next almost seemed like a miracle. She said, 'yes, I am damn upset... "and went on for another minute venting her anger. Then, almost at once, she relaxed and said, "I know it is not your fault, so let us see how we can solve this problem."

C. Be prepared for several "negative" questions. Listed below:

- What was the most difficult problem you had to overcome in your last job? How did you cope with it?
- Tell me about a time you had difficulty working with a boss or coworker. How did you handle the situation?
- Tell me about a difficult decision you had to make. What made it difficult and how did you go about resolving it?

8. Situational interviews

What are they like?

Situational interviews are quite different from typical face-to-face interviews. Instead of having a conversation, these interviews require you to perform a task. These tasks vary depending upon the technique used. There are four situational interviews you are most likely to encounter:

A. Group problem solving

You may be asked to sit at one of several tables, each table seating three to four other job seekers. You may be informed that each table represents a company team and that each team will have an hour to solve a certain problem. You will be given the details of the problem and your teams' discussion will be facilitated by a company representative (often a consultant or an HR employee).

B.   In-Basket

You will be given a box of memos, telephone messages, appointment schedules, project deadlines and assorted papers that typically come across a business manager's desk. Your task is to prioritise items in a short time, usually thirty to forty-five minutes.

Your prospective employer wants to observe your organisational skills, thought processes and analytical skills and ability to handle the stress of time pressure.

C.   Role-Play

You will be asked to perform a task such as making a sales presentation (usually you will be given product information and time to prepare). At other times, the role-play may involve your acting as a consultant, manager or customer service representative.

During role-play, observers try to evaluate your interpersonal skills and ability to handle difficult situations like those that will be encountered in real life. Usually, the situation will be an angry customer who has received bad service or a damaged product.

D.   Assessment centre

This method is used to evaluate many candidates for a particular job. If you are going to be evaluated by the assessment centre method, you will be informed in advance. One reason is that the evaluation process may be over a period of several days.

In most centres, you may encounter a variety of situational interviews, including a mixture of group problem solving, in-basket and role-play. Several observers will rate your performance.

How to succeed with situational interviews?

- You must recognise that situational interviews are really performances.
- Learn as much as you can about the prospective employer
- In group discussions, try to relax and be yourself

- Read about the techniques that situational interviewers make use of. Read about time management. But most important it is you and your abilities that will get you through.

Four Key Points to Remember

The four most important behaviours to concentrate on during an interview, missing just one of these four behaviours will cost you the job you are looking for:

1. **Do not over-verbalise**—Remember to be brief in whatever you say and to the point. As mentioned earlier, do not give any unnecessary information that was not asked of you or is irrelevant to the job and what they don't need to know.

2. **Be enthusiastic**—Exhibit energy and vitality and show the interviewers that you are an energetic person and not a lazy person. As an energetic person, you will complete your tasks fast, but as a lazy person they should expect delays in your work.

3. **Be positive**—Express clearly that you like what you see. Show them that you have a positive attitude to working for the organisation, and you will give your best to completing the work on time.

4. **Know your self**—Talk about your skills and strengths, express them with confidence. Show them that you have the capabilities to do the work that is required of you and that you are confident that with your abilities you can complete all assigned tasks.

Sources of Information

- Drake, John D.1997. "*The Perfect Interview*" *How to Get the Job You Really Want*, 2nd ed. Amacom American Management Association, New York.
- Saad E. Abbas 2007. "*How to Get the Right Job*" Department of Economic Development, Dubai.

4

The New Interviews Styles after COVID-19

The Changes That Have Taken Place in Interviews After COVID-19

The year 2020 is the year of many changes. The world actually went through a fantastic change. Something that has never happened before. Overnight, the world shutdown and started working from home. When people talk about the fourth Industrial revelation and when it started. In my book, it will always be 2020. The year the world changed and working from home became the new norm.

As the world changed so did the way interviews are conducted many large international organisations started interviewing people online. They said that we do not need to have the employees physically present at the headquarters of the company in whatever country. People can now stay in their own countries and work online. Reducing travel expenses, relocation expenses to a new country, VISA and passport issues removed. This also reduces travel time to and from work and money as now they will pay new employees in their own currency and not in Dollars or Euros.

Let us start with online interviews, the future is here, and we have to prepare ourselves for it.

Everyone is used to conduct face-to-face interviews, most of us may have a problem with conducting online interviews, talking infront of a camera may create anxiety for a lot of people. It is important to be prepared with the right knowledge for online interviews.

A.　What virtual meeting platforms you will be using?

Most organisations use the following platforms for all their meetings:

- Zoom
- Microsoft Teams
- Google Meet
- Cisco Webex

So, get acquainted with the platforms that you may be using for your online interview.

B.　Be on time

All platforms have a waiting area that when you log in you will be asked by the system to wait until you will be admitted by the host. It is recommended that you log in at least 15 minutes before the interview appointment. This way you will show the interviewers that you are a serious person and a person who values time. As they will be aware that you are in the waiting area as soon as you log in.

So be on time and be ready to start the interview before your anointed time as some interviews get concluded ahead of time.

C.　Check your surroundings before you log in

It is important to check your surroundings before the meeting starts. Make sure you turn the camera on before the meeting to see what the room behind you looks like. You may be surprised with what people can see behind you or around you. Sometimes you could have bad lighting people can't see your face. Sometimes the camera angle is incorrect where people can see the top half of your head or worse the top of your head. So, it is a good idea to check the camera before the meeting.

D.　Keep your eyes on the camera

During a meeting, it is very important to look at the camera when you are talking or giving a presentation. This is called creating eye contact with the other attendees. What most people do is they look at the videos of the other attendees. This makes them look strange and unfocused. If you are giving a presentation, then if you need to look at the presentation, just look at it briefly then shift your eyes back to the camera. Very important stop looking at yourself. Don't worry you look great.

The best way to look like you have eye contact with the other people in a virtual meeting is to sit at a distance from your computer I pad. So when you look at the screen, it appears that you have eye contact as the other people in the meeting cannot differentiate from you looking at the presentation looking at yourself or looking at them. Location as well as people or kids that can enter the screen range.

E.   Don't be a talking head

I have seen many virtual meetings with talking heads or talking half heads. Some people have a bad habit of not fixing the camera angle properly, so you end up seeing part of their head and the sealing. Also, it is important for people to see your neck and shoulders, this makes you appear more trustworthy and relaxed.

Also it is important to remember when gesturing with your hands always keep your hands close to your body don't stick your hands in front of the camera, this makes your hands look extremely large and it could distract people from the point you are making. It is important to keep your hands within the frame of the camera if you would like to show something big then your hands may stretch out of the camera frame this is not good. Try and always keep your hands close to your body and inside the camera frame.

F.   Have the right posture

Remember to always keep your shoulders back, also remember to put your arms in front of you this will make you look more confident, remember if you slouch during a virtual meeting, you will appear week and negative. It is important to always have a positive attitude.

Remember that when you are not talking people can still see you so be careful of the nonverbal communication. Some people tend to make facial expressions when listing to someone, these expressions could mean I don't like what you are saying like moving your eyes upward. Putting your hands on your mouth means What did you just say, and many more so be very careful with your expressions as people can see everything.

G.   Use headphones or earbuds

It is important to use headphones or earbuds. People usually ask me why should we use headphones or earbuds since they can talk, their voice is clear and they can hear clearly without headphones or earbuds? I tell them that when you do not use headphones or earbuds you create an echo. When a person is talking to a person who is not using headphones or earbuds this creates an echo. This is quite irritating to everyone in the interview. So please think of others as you are not the only person in the interview. Please use headphones or earbuds whatever you feel more comfortable with. My personal favourite is earbuds. I personally find it extremely comfortable. It is not bulky and heavy. What I have found is after some time headphones tend to feel heavy and give me a headache. The thing I like about headphones is that it blocks outside sound.

Sources of Information

- https://www.hightechpartners.net/blog/
  interviewing-in-times-of-covid-19-and-beyond
- https://www.siliconrepublic.com/advice/7-interview-questions-after- covid-19
- https://www.wsi.com/articles/what-to-wear-to-a-zoom-interview-and-other-
  style-dilemmas-solved-11601092812